SWAN, ERIN PEMBREY.
KANGAROOS AND KOALAS :
WHAT THEY HAVE OFFICIAL
2000. DISCARD
BRARY
10000679111408   5/02
WIND

11/22-3 S CKO

W9-BUA-778

Erin Pembrey Swan

Kangaroos and Koalas

What They Have in Common

Franklin Watts - A Division of Grolier Publishing
New York • London • Hong Kong • Sydney • Danbury, Connecticut

For Pete, just because

Photographs ©: Animals Animals: 22, 23 (B. Wells/OSF); BBC Natural History Unit: 25 (John Cancalosi); ENP Images: 5 bottom left, 31, 37, 42 (Gerry Ellis); NHPA: 39 (A.N.T), 27 (Pavel German); Peter Arnold Inc.: 5 bottom right, 6, 17, 19, 21 (John Cancalosi), 1 (Auscape/J. P. Ferrero), 13 (Gerard Lacz), 5 top left, 32, 33 (Roland Seitre); Photo Researchers: 40 (Bill Bachman), 41 (J. P. Ferrero/JACANA Scientific Control), 5 top right, 29 (Tom McHugh); Visuals Unlimited: 35 (Ken Lucas), 7 (Charles Philip), cover (Inga Spence); Wildlife Collection: 15 (Martin Harvey).

Illustrations by Jose Gonzales and Steve Savage

The photo on the cover shows a koala in a eucalyptus tree. The photo on the title page shows one red kangaroo standing guard while three others take a drink.

Visit Franklin Watts on the Internet at:
http://publishing.grolier.com

Library of Congress Cataloging-in-Publication Data

Swan, Erin Pembrey.
Kangaroos and koalas: what they have in common / Erin Pembrey Swan.
        p. cm. — (Animals in order)
    Includes bibliographical references and index.
    Summary: Describes the physical characteristics and behavior of fourteen species of diprotodonts, a primarily herbivorous order of marsupials, including possums, koalas, kangaroos, wallabies, and wombats.
        ISBN 0-531-11593-3 (lib. bdg.)   0-531-16447-0 (pbk.)
        1. Marsupialia Juvenile literature.   [1. Marsupials.] I. Title. II. Series.
QL737.M3S95   2000
599.2—dc21   99-15453
                                                                        CIP

GROLIER
PUBLISHING

©2000 Franklin Watts, A Division of Grolier Publishing
All rights reserved. Published simultaneously in Canada.
Printed in the United States of America.
1 2 3 4 5 6 7 8 9 10 R 09 08 07 06 05 04 03 02 01 00

Contents

What Is a Marsupial?

What does a huge animal hopping across the plains have in common with a round, furry creature nibbling leaves high in the treetops? This question is not a riddle. The answer is simple—they are both *marsupials*. One is a bouncing kangaroo, and the other is a tree-climbing koala. Marsupials are a kind of *mammal*.

A kangaroo and a koala also have something else in common—they both eat plants. That is why scientists place these animals in a special group, or *order*, called diprotodonts (DIH-proh-toh-DONTS). The word "diprotodont" means "two first teeth." The front teeth of a diprotodont are perfect for nipping and grinding tough plants.

There are many different plant-eating marsupials. Some are large, and some are small. Some live in grassy places, while others spend most of their time in the treetops. Three of the animals on the next page are plant-eating marsupials. One of them is not. Can you guess which one is not?

Sugar glider

Gopher

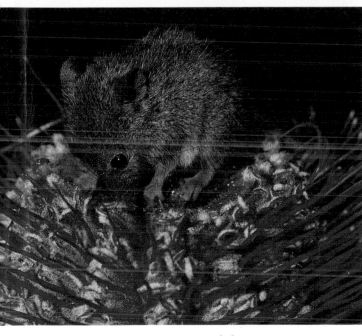

Honey possum

Wallaby

Traits of Plant-eating Marsupials

Did you guess the gopher? You were right! How can you tell it is not a plant-eating marsupial? All marsupials have one important thing in common—the way their babies are born.

A baby gopher, like most other baby mammals, grows inside its mother and is born fully formed. A baby marsupial is born before it has finished developing. It clings to its mother's fur and climbs up her body until it reaches a pouch on her belly. Once inside, the tiny

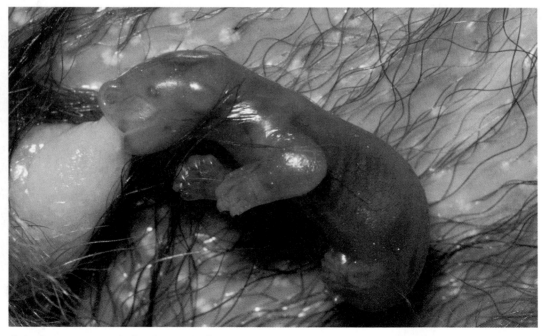

A baby marsupial drinks milk from its mother's mammary gland.

marsupial attaches itself to its mother's *mammary gland* and stays there for many months. During that time, it drinks its mother's milk. When the marsupial grows big enough, it leaves its mother's pouch. For the next few months, the baby spends some time in the world, but it climbs back into its mother's pouch when it feels hungry or scared.

Plant-eating marsupials have just one pair of teeth in their lower jaw, and most have three pairs of teeth on top. They don't need as many teeth as people do because most of the time they eat plants. A few eat some insects and small mammals.

A young kangaroo climbs inside its mother's pouch when it is hungry or scared.

The Order of Living Things

A tiger has more in common with a house cat than with a daisy. A true bug is more like a butterfly than a jellyfish. Scientists arrange living things into groups based on how they look and how they act. A tiger and a house cat belong to the same group, but a daisy belongs to a different group.

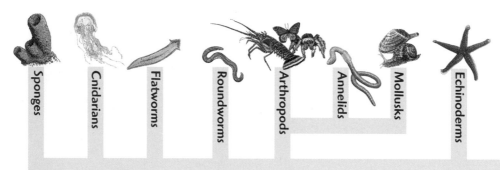

Sponges · Cnidarians · Flatworms · Roundworms · Arthropods · Annelids · Mollusks · Echinoderms

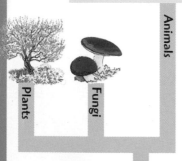

Plants · Fungi · Animals

Monerans · Protists

All living things can be placed in one of five groups called *kingdoms*: the plant kingdom, the animal kingdom, the fungus kingdom, the moneran kingdom, or the protist kingdom. You can probably name many of the creatures in the plant and animal kingdoms. The fungus kingdom includes mushrooms, yeasts, and molds. The moneran and protist kingdoms contain thousands of living things that are too small to see without a microscope.

8

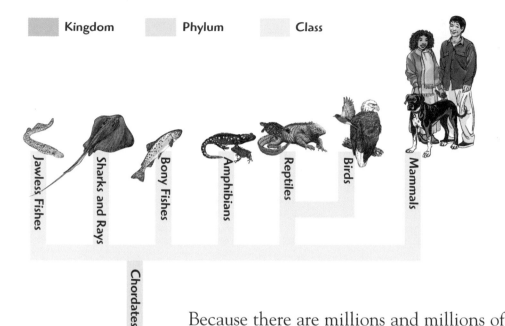

Kingdom   Phylum   Class

Jawless Fishes

Sharks and Rays

Bony Fishes

Amphibians

Reptiles

Birds

Mammals

Chordates

Because there are millions and millions of living things on Earth, some of the members of one kingdom may not seem all that similar. The animal kingdom includes creatures as different as tarantulas and trout, jellyfish and jaguars, salamanders and sparrows, elephants and earthworms.

To show that an elephant is more like a jaguar than an earthworm, scientists further separate the creatures in each kingdom into more specific groups. The animal kingdom can be divided into nine *phyla*. Humans belong to the chordate phylum. Almost all chordates have a backbone.

Each phylum can be subdivided into many *classes*. Humans, mice, and elephants all belong to the mammal class. Each class can be further divided into orders; orders into *families*, families into *genera*, and genera into *species*. All the members of a species are very similar.

9

How Plant-eating Marsupials Fit In

You can probably guess that plant-eating marsupials belong to the animal kingdom. They have much more in common with bees and bats than with maple trees and morning glories.

Plant-eating marsupials belong to the chordate phylum. Almost all chordates have a backbone and a skeleton. Can you think of other chordates? Examples include lions, mice, snakes, birds, fish, and whales.

The chordate phylum is divided into several classes. Plant-eating marsupials belong to the mammal class. Mice, whales, dogs, cats, and humans are all mammals.

There are seventeen orders of mammals. Plant-eating marsupials make up one of the two orders of marsupials. They live in Australia, New Guinea, Tasmania, and other nearby islands. Most live in trees, but some roam the wide plains and deserts. One plant-eating marsupial—the wombat—lives underground.

The plant-eating marsupials can be divided into a number of different families. Each family is divided into a number of different genera and species. In this book, you will learn more about some of the plant-eating marsupials.

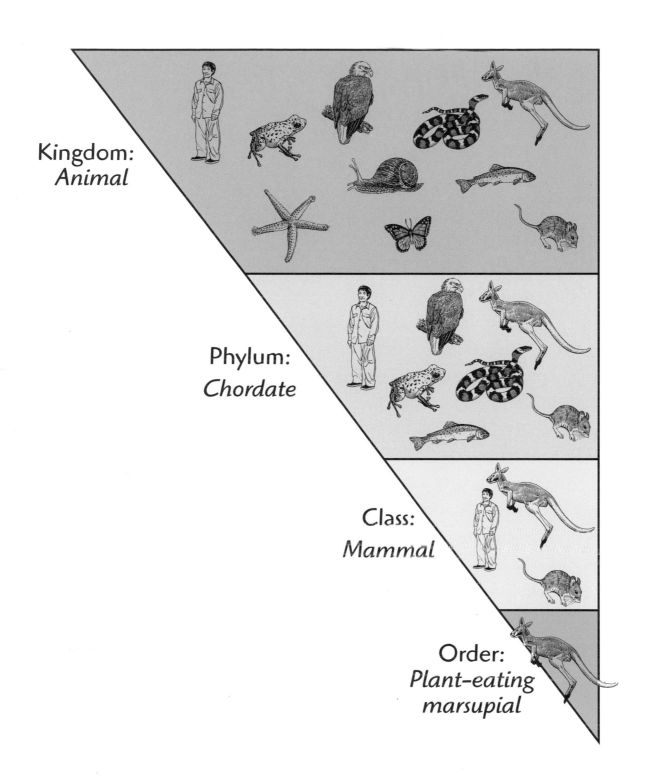

Kingdom:
Animal

Phylum:
Chordate

Class:
Mammal

Order:
*Plant-eating
marsupial*

Kangaroos

FAMILY: Macropodidae
COMMON EXAMPLE: Red kangaroo
GENUS AND SPECIES: *Macropus rufus*
SIZE: 57 inches (145 cm)

A *mob* of red kangaroos grazes on a hot grassy plain in Australia. They move slowly on all fours, munching grass with their strong, flat teeth. Here and there, a young kangaroo, called a *joey*, pokes its head out of its mother's pouch.

A newborn joey is about the size of your fingertip. It spends about 8 months growing in its mother's pouch before it hops out for the first time. For a few months after that, it returns once in a while for food or safety, or just to get a free ride.

Kangaroos move slowly most of the time, but they can move very fast when they want to. A kangaroo's back legs are very strong and perfect for jumping. When they sense danger, kangaroos can bound along at 40 miles (64 km) per hour. They can cover 25 feet (7.5 m) in a single jump and leap more than 6 feet (1.8 m) high!

Kangaroos live in Australia, New Guinea, and some small islands nearby. In hot weather, they lick their paws to keep cool. Kangaroos get most of the water they need from the plants they eat, so they do not need to drink water very often. If a *dingo* or other animal tries to attack a kangaroo, it kicks the enemy with its powerful back legs. This can hurt—or even kill—the attacker.

13

Wombats

FAMILY: Vombatidae
COMMON EXAMPLE: Common wombat
GENUS AND SPECIES: *Vombatus ursinus*
SIZE: 28 to 47 inches (71 to 119 cm)

The hot Australian day is just beginning. A coarse-haired wombat waddles home to its *burrow*. During the night, it fed on grasses and roots. The wombat disappears into a maze of underground tunnels, where it will sleep the day away.

Wombats look a little like bears. They have heavy bodies and short legs. They use their strong, clawed forefeet to dig deep into the earth. Their heads are perfect for pushing dirt out of the way. Some wombat burrows are very simple, but others have many rooms and more than one entrance. Some of their burrows are more than 100 feet (30 m) long.

When the weather is hot, wombats sleep all day in their cool burrows, and come out at night to feed. Wombats eat roots, bark, and grasses. They also nibble on *fungi*. Wombats that live near the coast sometimes search for fish or crabs along the beach.

Wombats like company. They often visit each other's burrows, just as people visit their neighbors' homes. What a friendly way to live!

Quokkas
FAMILY: Macropodidae
COMMON NAME: Quokka
GENUS AND SPECIES: *Setonix brackyurus*
SIZE: 19 to 23 inches (48 to 58 cm)

The cool evening has finally come after a long, hot summer day. A quokka pokes its bald nose out of a shady *thicket* and sniffs the air. Yum! The quokka can smell juicy grass just waiting to be eaten. Quickly, it hops out into the dry clearing to find it.

The quokka is a small wallaby that lives mostly in the dense, moist swamps of southwestern Australia. Although it likes cool, damp places best, the quokka can live in hot, dry places, too. These marsupials are common on Rottnest Island and Bald Island, off the coast of Australia.

Like a kangaroo, a quokka has strong back legs. It can hop quickly if it wants to. Most of the time, a quokka grazes on all fours or scampers through the tunnels it has made in the thick under-brush. A quokka gets moisture from the grasses it eats, so it can go a long time without drinking water.

Quokkas live in family groups. The biggest, strongest adult male is in charge. These animals usually live peacefully together. They often appear in groups at dawn and dusk to share some tasty clumps of grass.

Wallabies
FAMILY: Macropodidae
COMMON EXAMPLE: Tammar wallaby
GENUS AND SPECIES: *Macropus exigent*
SIZE: 20 to 26 1/2 inches (50 to 67 cm)

A young tammar wallaby pokes its head out of the pouch on its mother's belly. Although it weighed about as much as a paper clip when it was born, this joey is now almost big enough to hop about by itself.

After 8 or 9 months of growing in its mother's warm, deep pouch, a young wallaby is ready to come out and explore. For a few more months, it will return to the pouch when it is hungry or scared. But when it learns to eat grass like a grown-up, a young wallaby is ready for life on its own.

Like the red kangaroo, a wallaby is a species of kangaroo. Although it is smaller, the wallaby has strong back legs that are perfect for jumping. If it is attacked by an enemy, such as a dingo or a hawk, a wallaby will quickly leap away to safety. If it doesn't have time to escape, the wallaby can balance on its powerful tail and kick out fiercely with its back legs. Those strong legs and sharp claws usually drive an enemy away.

Wallabies live in thick, shrubby areas in Australia and New Guinea. They travel at night in mobs of up to fifty wallabies. The bigger males are usually in charge and often fight other males to

18

stay in power. When two males fight, each one grabs at the other with its front legs and kicks with its back legs. The wallaby who gives up first loses the battle.

Pademelons

FAMILY: Macropodidae
COMMON EXAMPLE: Tasmanian pademelon
GENUS AND SPECIES: *Thylogale billardierii*
SIZE: 19 1/2 inches (50 cm)

It is a hot sunny day in Tasmania, an island off the southeast coast of Australia. A Tasmanian pademelon rests inside its burrow—a tunnel in the dense underbrush. When evening comes, and the air cools down, the pademelon will leave its burrow to feed on grasses, shrubs, and tree saplings.

Pademelons are in the same family as kangaroos and wallabies. In fact, they are sometimes called "shrub wallabies." They hop on their strong back legs when they need to, but spend most of their time grazing on all four feet.

Some pademelons live in small groups, while others live alone. When they aren't feeding, they rest and *groom* each other. Mothers and their young spend a lot of time grooming each other's thick, soft fur.

Female pademelons give birth in the fall and winter. The tiny newborns grow in their mother's pouch for about 7 months. The babies come out in spring when there is plenty of food to eat. Young pademelons grow quickly. They're ready to have their own babies when they are only 14 months old!

Honey Possums

FAMILY: Tarsipedidae
COMMON NAME: Honey possum
GENUS AND SPECIES: *Tarsipes rostratus*
SIZE: 2 3/4 to 3 1/4 inches (7 to 8 cm)

Honey possums don't really eat honey, but they do love sweet things. This little animal, which is sometimes called a noolbender, uses its strong tail to hang upside down from the branches of flowering trees. It grabs blossoms with its front paws, and sticks its long tongue deep inside. Tiny bristles on the possum's tongue tip gather the flower's sweet *nectar*. When a honey possum pulls its tongue in, the nectar slides down its throat. Delicious!

Honey possums like pollen and nectar best, but they also eat insects that live inside the flowers they feed from. A honey possum's head is perfectly shaped for feeding on the nectar and pollen deep inside the flowers.

22

Its pointed snout is long and narrow, and its special brush-tipped tongue is one-third as long as its whole body!

Baby honey possums are usually born in autumn, spring, and early summer when most trees are blossoming, and there is plenty to eat. Newborn honey possums are the smallest of all newborn mammals. They weigh less than half an aspirin tablet. Can you imagine a mammal that small?

Koalas

FAMILY: Phascolarctidae
COMMON NAME: Koala
GENUS AND SPECIES: *Phascolarctos cinereus*
SIZE: 24 to 33 inches (61 to 84 cm)

A female koala rests on a tree branch and munches on juicy *eucalyptus* leaves. Her baby clings to her fuzzy belly. After spending 7 months in its mother's pouch, the baby is just learning to live in the world. When the mother is ready to move on, the little koala crawls onto her back. It clings to its mother's soft, thick fur as she climbs about in search of more leaves.

A koala may look like a teddy bear, but it is a marsupial. It has a large nose, round ears, and no tail. Koalas have to eat a lot to keep up their energy. Each koala eats more than 20 pounds (9 kg) of eucalyptus leaves in 1 day!

These furry little creatures live in the eucalyptus forests of Australia and the islands nearby. They sleep most of the day and look for food at night. Koalas are good climbers, but they are very slow. They stay in the trees most of the time. They come to the ground only to get from one tree to the next. Because a koala's diet is so low in energy, they need to rest a lot. A koala may sleep up to 18 hours a day!

Adult koalas spend time together during mating season, but most of the time they live alone. Except for females with their young, there is usually only one koala per tree.

If a koala feels threatened, it simply climbs to a safer place. It stores unchewed leaves in its cheek pouches until it finds a place where it can rest safely.

Glider Possums

FAMILY: Pseudocheiridae
COMMON EXAMPLE: Great glider possum
GENUS AND SPECIES: *Petauroides volans*
SIZE: 3 to 4 inches (7 to 10 cm)

A great glider possum nibbles on the juicy new leaves of a eucalyptus tree. When the possum can't find any more to eat, it runs to the end of the branch, leaps off, and glides through the air. Folds of skin between its elbows and ankles stretch out like parachutes so it doesn't fall. As it lands on another tree trunk, the possum digs its claws into the bark to hold on.

A great glider possum can glide more than 330 feet (100 m) from one tree to another. What a wonderful way to travel through the forest!

These little possums live in the eucalyptus forests of Australia and New Guinea. They build leafy nests in tree hollows. During the day, they curl up in tight, fluffy balls and sleep. At night, they wake up and sniff the air. All kinds of good smells are carried on the breeze. They scamper out and glide through the treetops in search of tasty eucalyptus blossoms and new leaf buds.

Great glider possums like to live alone in the trees. Males and females share a nest only during breeding season. A female gives birth to only one baby at a time. It grows quickly and is soon a big-eared, fluffy glider possum like its parents.

Pygmy Possums

FAMILY: Burramyidae
COMMON EXAMPLE: Eastern pygmy possum
GENUS AND SPECIES: *Cercaertetus nanus*
SIZE: 4 1/2 to 11 1/2 inches (11 to 29 cm)

High on a tree branch, a tiny eastern pygmy possum pokes its little mouse like head out of its nest and looks around. It is August, and the Australian winter is finally over. After long months of lying still and quiet in its leafy nest, this possum is ready to scamper through the forest once again. It crawls out of its nest and scurries along the tree branch. It is looking for flowers to feed on. The pollen and nectar from the blossoms make tasty treats for this small possum.

Pygmy possums are active from early spring to late fall. They run through the trees at night, eating insects and drinking nectar from eucalyptus blossoms. During the day, they curl up in their nests and sleep. They build their nests on tree branches or in hollows. Sometimes a pygmy possum moves into an old bird's nest.

Most pygmy possums live alone, but during the winter two or more share a nest. They stay very still during the cold months, using the fat stored in their tails for energy. That way they don't have to go out into the cold to find food.

Pygmy possums mate in spring. Each mother gives birth to four or five young. The tiny helpless newborns grow inside the mother's pouch until they're big enough to live on their own.

Tree Kangaroos

FAMILY: Macropodidae

COMMON EXAMPLE: Goodfellow's tree
   kangaroo

GENUS AND SPECIES: *Dendrolagus goodfellowi*

SIZE: 21 1/2 to 24 inches (54.5 to 61 cm)

In the early evening, a tree kangaroo shakes itself awake. It perches on a branch high in the treetops and looks down at the dense rain forest below. After a long day of sleeping, this little kangaroo is very hungry.

The small kangaroo uses its strong back legs to bound from one branch to the next. The animal's tail helps it balance. When it reaches the ground, it hops about on all fours. It is looking for grass, fruit, and flowers to eat.

Tree kangaroos live in the rain forests of Australia and New Guinea. They spend most of their time alone. They sleep in trees during the day and feed on the ground at night. They have strong front and back legs, so they hop easily from tree to tree. A tree kangaroo can leap up to 60 feet (18 m) from a tree to the ground!

Just before a female tree kangaroo gives birth, she licks her pouch clean to make it ready for the tiny baby. When the baby is born, it crawls into the mother's pouch and grows there for almost 1 year. Even after a young kangaroo leaves the mother's pouch, it climbs back in when it is hungry or just needs a rest.

30

Rat-Kangaroos

FAMILY: Macropodidae

COMMON EXAMPLE: Musky rat-kangaroo

GENUS AND SPECIES: *Hypsiprymnodon moschatus*

SIZE: 8 to 13 inches (20 to 33 cm)

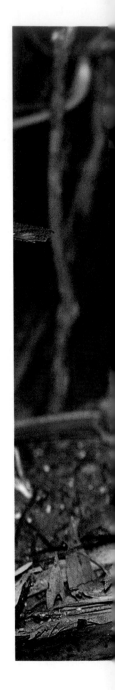

Musky rat-kangaroos live in the rain forests of Queensland, Australia. They get their name from their strong, musky scent.

During the day, musky rat-kangaroos dash through the dense underbrush on all fours. They spend most of their time alone, but sometimes they feed together in groups of two or three.

When a musky rat-kangaroo is hungry, it digs into the damp soil of the rain forest. It uses its small claws to turn over leaves and dirt as it looks for food. When it finds a tasty treat, the rat-kangaroo sits back on its haunches and nibbles its dinner. These small rat-like animals eat all kinds of foods. They like earthworms, roots, insects, and berries.

At night rat-kangaroos crawl into their nests and sleep. They make their nests in the forks between tree branches or in dense bushes. Their naked, scaly tails are perfect for gathering the dried grasses, ferns, and *lichens* they use to build their nests.

Female rat-kangaroos usually give birth to two babies at a time. After 5 months in their mother's pouch, the young are big enough to go out on their own.

Sugar Gliders

FAMILY: Petauridae
COMMON NAME: Sugar glider
GENUS AND SPECIES: *Petaurus breviceps*
SIZE: 5 to 7 inches (12.5 to 18 cm)

Whoosh! A sugar glider leaps from a tree branch, and the thin folds of skin between its feet and ankles stretch out. The little animal glides safely to another tree. A sugar glider steers with its fluffy tail. That way, it can land exactly where it wants to.

Sugar gliders live in the forests of northern and eastern Australia. During the day, they sleep in nests made of leaves and twigs. At night, they look for food.

Sugar gliders get their name from all the sweet things they eat. They like to sip nectar and eat pollen from flowers. They also lap up the sugary sap of eucalyptus trees. They eat insects, too—especially moths and beetles.

These little animals move easily through the trees. They glide from branch to branch like tiny flying squirrels. A sugar glider can travel up to 150 feet (45.5 m) in a single glide!

Small family groups of up to seven sugar gliders live together in the forests. One male glider is the leader of the group. He marks the area where the group lives with a special scent made inside his body. He also sprays each member of his group. Then, if a different-smelling stranger enters their area, the sugar gliders quickly chase it away.

34

Cuscuses

FAMILY: Phalangeridae
COMMON EXAMPLE: Spotted cuscus
GENUS AND SPECIES: *Spilocuscus maculates*
SIZE: 20 inches (51 cm)

A male spotted cuscus moves slowly along a branch in the Australian rain forest. He grips the branch with the rough underside of his *prehensile tail*. This helps him keep his balance as he looks for tasty leaves and fruits to munch on. He might even catch a lizard or bird to go with his fruit and vegetables.

These small-eared, woolly creatures live most of their lives in the trees. They hardly ever come down to the ground. Cuscuses sleep the hot day away perched comfortably among the tree branches. When the cool evening comes, they wake up and groom their thick fur with their claws. All night they roam the treetops looking for good things to eat.

Most cuscuses live in New Guinea, but a few live in Australia. Some of the males have colorful yellow or orange stripes or spots. Females are usually gray and white. A cuscus's coat may change color a few times during its life.

The male cuscus can be very tough. He marks his territory with a scent and defends his area fiercely. Even a female is fierce if an enemy attacks—barking, snarling, and striking out with her claws. For such small animals, cuscuses can be very dangerous!

Bettongs

FAMILY: Potoroidae
EXAMPLE: Northern bettong
GENUS AND SPECIES: *Bettongia tropica*
SIZE: 15 inches (38 cm)

A bettong hops slowly along the forest floor searching for good things to eat. Suddenly it spots a hungry dingo! The bettong hops away from the wild dog as fast as its strong back legs can carry it. Luckily, the bettong moves faster than the dingo. It dives into the underbrush and is safe.

Bettongs can be found only on the edges of rain forests in the northeastern part of Queensland, Australia. Even though these small marsupials breed all year round, their numbers are still very low.

During the day, bettongs curl up in cozy nests hidden in clumps of grass. They have a lot of enemies, so they need a safe place to sleep. Dingoes, wild cats, and pigs will all eat any bettongs they can catch.

At night, bettongs look for food. Their favorite food is truffles—fungi that grow underground. Bettongs dig up truffles with their small front paws and munch happily on the earthy treat. Bettongs eat many other things, too. Grass roots, seeds, herbs, and lilies are all food to a hungry bettong.

Will Plant-eating Marsupials Survive?

In the past, plant-eating marsupials were common in Australia, New Guinea, and Tasmania. In recent years, however, they have become more and more rare. In fact, some of them are now *endangered species*. They are in danger of dying out completely.

A few hundred years ago, people from Europe began to settle in Australia and islands nearby. They built houses and roads and, eventually, cities. They raised cattle and sheep—animals that eat a lot of grass and need a lot of space.

A ranch in Australia

These people and their farm animals began to take over the *habitats* of many plant-eating marsupials. When they cut down rain forest trees for lumber, they destroyed the homes of cuscuses and tree kangaroos. When they fenced off feeding grounds for their farm animals, they took food and space away from red kangaroos and wombats.

European settlers also began hunting plant-eating marsupials. Native people had hunted these animals too, but they hadn't killed enough of them to put the animals in danger of disappearing.

Europeans hunted plant-eating marsupials for many different reasons. Kangaroos were, and still are, hunted for their meat and hide. They were also killed because they ate the grasses people wanted to feed their farm animals. Wombats were hunted for their fur. Koalas, wallabies, pademelons, and cuscuses were hunted for their meat and their fur. Some plant-eating marsupials were hunted for "sport."

People still hunt kangaroos.

Kangaroos and wallabies get infected teeth and gums from eating soft food like bread, biscuits and sweets. Many die of "lumpy jaw", a killer disease that starts in infected gums.

Please feed them fresh vegetable matter only.

TASMANIA
NATIONAL PARKS & WILDLIFE SERVICE

This red-necked wallaby lives in a national park in Tasmania.

For all these reasons, certain species of plant-eating marsupials have vanished completely from parts of Australia. The koala and the brush-tailed bettong disappeared from southern Australia about 100 years ago. Because some animals were brought back to this area from Victoria and western Australia, koalas and bettongs now thrive again in the south.

People have made other efforts to save plant-eating marsupials. National parks provide protected areas for many animals. New laws make it illegal to hunt many of them. As a result, some plant-eating marsupials have been saved.

But others, such as the bettong, are still in danger. Kangaroos are killed because they eat grasses from rancher's fields. Other plant-eating marsupials are hunted for their meat and hides.

People are trying to save plant-eating marsupials, but much more needs to be done. How sad it would be if these ancient and fascinating animals disappeared from our planet!

Words to Know

burrow—a shelter dug in the ground

class—a group of creatures within a phylum that share certain characteristics

endangered species—a plant or animal species that is in danger of disappearing from Earth.

eucalyptus—a kind of tree that grows in Australia. Some eucalyptus trees give off a gummy substance.

dingo—a wild dog found in Australia

family—a group of creatures within an order that share certain characteristics

fungus (plural fungi)—a living thing that is neither a plant nor an animal. Mushrooms and toadstools are fungi.

genus (plural genera)—a group of creatures within a family that share certain characteristics

groom—to pick dirt and insects out of fur

habitat—the place where a plant or animal lives and grows

joey—a young marsupial

kingdom—one of the five divisions into which all living things are placed: the animal kingdom, the plant kingdom, the fungus kingdom, the moneran kingdom, and the protist kingdom

lichen—a mosslike growth that lives on rocks and trees. It is made up of a fungus and algae.

mammal—an animal that has a backbone and feeds its young with mother's milk

mammary gland—the part of a female mammal's body that produces milk for its young

marsupial—a mammal that is born in an early stage of development and grows in its mother's pouch

nectar—a sugary liquid made by plants. It attracts animals that will carry the plants' pollen from one flower to another.

mob—a group, or herd, of kangaroos or similar marsupials

order—a group of creatures within a class that share certain characteristics

phylum (plural **phyla**)—a group of creatures within a kingdom that shares certain characteristics

prehensile tail—a tail that can be used for grabbing and grasping

species—a group of creatures within a genus that share certain characteristics. Members of a species can mate and produce young.

thicket—land covered with dense shrubs and vines

Learning More

Books

Arnold, Caroline. *Koala*. New York: Mulberry Books, 1992.

Atkinson, Kathie. *Outback Animals*. St. Leonardo, Australia: Allen & Unwin, 1994.

Crewe, Sabrina. *The Kangaroos*. Chatham, NJ: Raintree Steck-Vaughn, 1998.

Jansen, John and Susan Burke Slattery. *Playing Possum: Riddles About Kangaroos, Koalas, and Other Marsupials*. Minneapolis, MN: Lerner, 1995.

Marko, Katherine McGlade. *Pocket Babies*. New York: Franklin Watts, 1995.

Triggs, Barbara. *The Wombat: Common Animals in Australia*. Portland, OR: International Specialized Book Service, 1996.

Web Sites

The Marsupial Museum
http://www.worldkids.net/critters/marsupials/
Learn all about cuscuses, kangaroos, quokkas, wombats, and other marsupials.

The Australian Mammal Society
http://ikarus.jcu.edu.au/mammal
This site was created and is maintained by James Cook University in Queensland, Australia. You can see photos and learn all about a wide variety of marsupials.

Index

About the Author

Erin Pembrey Swan studied animal behavior, literature, and early childhood education at Hampshire College in Massachusetts. She also studied literature and history at University College Galway in Ireland. Her poetry has been published in *The Poet's Gallery: The Subterraneans* and *The Poet's Gallery: Voices of Selene* in Woodstock, New York, and *The Cuirt Journal* in Galway, Ireland. Ms. Swan is also the author of *Primates: From Howler Monkeys to Humans*, *Land Predators of North America*, and *Camels and Pigs: What They Have in Common*. Although she lives in New Paltz, New York, Ms. Swan spends a great deal of time traveling.